Old Kilbarchan

John Hood

This is most probably the Milliken Mill, of which little other than the weir and sluices now remains. It was erected on the banks of the Black Cart, in what would later become the district of Milliken Park. The latter, once described as being 'at the mutual border of Kilbarchan and Abbey-Paisley parishes', was a thriving little community, with its own railway station on the Glasgow–Paisley–Kilmarnock–Ayr line. Mostly residential, Milliken Park comprised a number of magnificent eighteenth and nineteenth century villas designed by well-known Scottish architects. Notable residents included Archibald McLaurin (a partner in the firm of Smith & McLaurin, whose paper mill was nearby) and Matthew Anderson, who was said to be 'one of the best known personalities in the village'. A partner in Messrs Hetherington & Anderson, wool and yarn merchants, Glasgow, he was also very active in village affairs, chairing, for example, the committees appointed to raise funds for the new parish church and for the erection of a war memorial.

Text © John Hood, 2010.
First published in the United Kingdom, 2010,
by Stenlake Publishing Ltd.
Telephone: 01290 551122
www.stenlake.co.uk

ISBN 9781840335033

**The publishers regret that they cannot supply
copies of any pictures featured in this book.**

Acknowledgements

I would like to thank the following for their help: Maisie Brown, John Butler, Martin Cherrie, Alex Harrison, Andrew Henderson, Betty McDonald, Margaret Smith and David Weir (Reference & Local Studies Librarian, Renfrewshire Council). Finally, I should like to thank Helen Calcluth and Ian Trushell for reading through and commenting on the manuscript, although ultimately, of course, the responsibility for any errors or omissions remains mine.

The publisher and author wish to thank the following for permission to reproduce photographs in this book: Kilbarchan Civic Society for pages 15, 22, 25, 31, 44 and 46; Mrs Betty McDonald for pages 18, 23 (left) and 32; and Ms Sharon Duffy for page 24 (left).

Further Reading

The books listed below were used by the author during his research. None of them are available from Stenlake Publishing. Those interested in finding out more are advised to contact their local bookshop or local studies library.

Anderson, John Fyfe, *Kilbarchan in Old Picture Postcards*, European Library, Zaltbommel, 1989.
Brotchie, A.W. and Grieves, R.L., *Paisley's Trams and Buses: Twenties to Eighties*, N.B. Traction, Dundee, 1988.
Burgess, Moira, *Discover Kilbarchan, Bridge of Weir, Houston*, Renfrew District Council, 1995.
Moisley, H.A. and Thain, A.G., eds., *The Third Statistical Account of Scotland: The County of Renfrew*, Collins, Glasgow, 1962.

Introduction

There are two schools of thought regarding the derivation of the name 'Kilbarchan'. One is that it takes its name from St Barchan, a seventh century Irish saint, who appears to have had a tenuous link with the village. The other view is that 'Kilbarchan' means the church in the valley among the hills. There is, however, no dispute that, until 1560, the village of Kilbarchan and the surrounding lands came under the jurisdiction of Paisley Abbey. At that period, and until later industrialisation, the main occupation in the area was agriculture. However, as the 1695 Poll Tax records show, there were trades being practised locally, such as masonry, carpentry, tailoring and blacksmithing. Some other inhabitants were employed in one of the several corn mills which were situated along the banks of the Gryffe and Cart rivers, or in the mining of coal, freestone and lime at various localities throughout the parish.

The transformation of the old medieval village of Kilbarchan, however, began around 1739, when Kilbarchan-born Baillie John Barbour opened his Kilbarchan Linen Manufactury at the Stack Yard. This could produce greater quantities of good quality linen cloth than could the thirty to forty hand loom weavers then living and working in the village. Such was the success of Barbour's business that expansion into Ireland soon followed. This resulted in shipments of good quality Ulster flax being brought into the village, which further increased the local linen production. After John Barbour's death in 1770 the business was carried on by his three sons, John, William and Humphrey, two of whom branched out into the production of candles. Linen manufacture continued to expand, and by 1782 there were 360 looms operating in the village – most of the weaving in fact still being done on individual hand looms in the weaver's workshops, or in weaving sheds behind the houses. By 1836, the weaving industry peaked locally, with 800 looms providing sufficient work to support a population of 4,806. However, the gradual introduction of power looms, which were both quicker and cheaper, led to a steady decline in locally produced cloth. Although the Kilbarchan weavers later diversified into the production of tartans (and ponchos for the South American market!), the end was in sight and by 1900 the numbers of looms in the village had fallen to 200. Despite plans in 1948 for the revival of the industry, the number of working looms continued to fall, so that by 1953 there were fewer than five in the village.

Prior to 1700, Kilbarchan had been little more than a 'kirktoun' largely centred around the old parish church in the then High Street (now Church Street), but with industrialisation and the gaining of the status of Burgh of Barony, new streets were laid out, radiating from the Cross and the Steeple Building. Because of the speed of this expansion, these streets were typically narrow and lacked pavements, street lighting, and any form of drainage. The houses were generally two storeys high, with working space for the weavers on the ground floor and living quarters on the upper floor. As, typically, the families were living in cramped conditions and drawing water for drinking and washing from the several public wells, it is not surprising that epidemics of diseases such as measles and scarlet fever were rife. Gradually, however, the situation improved. In 1846, a gasworks was established at Low Barholm to supply the village with gas for lighting, and in 1881 the village finally gained a water supply when the Kilbarchan, Linwood and Brookfield special water supply was inaugurated by Mrs Finlayson of Merchiston House. Around the beginning of the twentieth century, the opening of a station at Low Barholm brought the railways to Kilbarchan. Transport links to and from the village were further enhanced when the Paisley & District tramway system was extended to Kilbarchan in 1907. The latter development was particularly significant, as it brought many visitors into the village (where they marvelled at its 'olde world' charm), thus creating a mini tourist boom. As the twentieth century progressed, however, this charm came under increasing threat, as the limitations of the old, narrow, streets and the housing on them, became more and more apparent. In 1938, for example, Clearance Orders were brought forward by the County Council, partly to demolish some of the older and, in their view, 'uninhabitable' houses in Shuttle Street and New Street, but also to open up the area around the Cross. This was resisted locally and, by and large, wasn't proceeded with. However, in the early 1960s, many of the older properties which had previously been identified for demolition were ultimately demolished, despite strong local opposition.

Further changes to the traditional appearance of the village were made in the 1970s when the Barn Green relief road was formed. Since then, however, Kilbarchan's designation as a Conservation Area has largely prevented any further demolition. In 1992, an Outstanding Conservation Area Enhancement Scheme was approved by Renfrew District Council to further protect the village's unique character. Today, Kilbarchan is largely a dormitory suburb, with fast links to Paisley, Glasgow and Greenock via the Johnstone bypass, which was opened in June 1992.

Milliken Park Arch. Kilbarchan.

In the early 1930s, the centrepiece of the annual Lilias Day celebrations was the series of magnificent floral arches that stretched from one side of the street to the other. This one, built for the 1933 event, was located near the Old Toll and was one of five such arches located at key points throughout the village, the others being at the Kirk-toun (now Church Street), Ewing Street, Shuttle Street and New Street. The construction of the arches was the responsibility of separate committees, each with their own convenor. The arches were built by the villagers using heather and whin branches, with additional features picked out with flowers. In addition to the arches, many of the houses bordering the parade route were festooned with flags and bunting. In 1933, the celebrations commenced with a grand parade of characters associated with Kilbarchan's past, followed by a historical pageant in the public park, devised by well-known local artist, James Wright. Around 30,000 visitors (some coming from abroad) attended the celebrations that year.

A Paisley & District tram proceeds along Easwald Bank, *en route* to the tram terminus at the Trust Inn. As can be seen, the line was single track, so that passing points were required at various locations. To the left of the photograph is Burnside Terrace, which takes its name from the Kilbarchan Burn which runs parallel with it. Rising within the Glentyan Estate, the burn now flows under Station Road, past the site of the old Kilbarchan Friendly Societies Joint Stock Gas Light Company, before crossing Easwald Bank, and passing into the former estate of James Milliken, where it was diverted to form a series of man-made waterfalls. In earlier years, power from the burn was harnessed for various commercial enterprises, including the Glentyan Corn Mill and the Glentyan Laundry Company. The latter was located within Merchant's Close and was run by Robert Gibson & Sons from about 1900 until the late 1920s, when Gibson left the company. Thereafter, the Glentyan Laundry was run by James McVicar, whilst Gibson established a new laundry company (the Cartbank Laundry) behind the Cartside Mill.

Until 1905, the nearest railway station to Kilbarchan was at Milliken Park. However, in that year the situation changed when a station was opened at Kilbarchan on a new 13.5 mile long 'loop line', which left the main Glasgow–Paisley–Kilmarnock–Ayr line at Elderslie's Cart Junction, before rejoining the main line at Brownhill Junction, near Dalry. The new station comprised an island platform, with booking hall and waiting rooms. Passenger access to and from the station platform was from Station Road, or via a sloping tunnel, the entrance and exit to which was formed in one of the supports of the railway bridge which carried the line over Low Barholm. Although initially well used, increasing competition from road transport eventually led to the withdrawal of passenger services. Finally, on 27 June 1966, the station itself was closed as a result of the Beeching cuts. The line continued to be used for freight until 3 July 1972, after which date the line was lifted. In the late 1980s, the path of the old line became part of the National Cycle Network and links Paisley, Johnstone, Lochwinnoch and the Ayrshire coast.

Official Opening by Board of Trade of Kilbarchan Tram Line from Johnstone.
Special Car driven by Mrs Houston.

On the afternoon of Wednesday, 5 July 1907, crowds gathered at Low Barholm, alongside the Trust Inn (on the extreme right of the photograph), to witness the arrival of a fleet of trams carrying officials and invited guests for the official opening of the Kilbarchan extension of the Paisley & District Tramway system. Driving one of these trams was Mrs Houston, the wife of one of the area's most prominent landowners. Although the arrival of the trams was clearly welcomed, the reception in Kilbarchan was rather more subdued than that at Barrhead, where an extension had opened earlier in the day. This was due to an ongoing local dispute in Kilbarchan about the location of the tram terminus – the villagers' preference was that it be sited at the entrance to Station Road, near the gates to the Glentyan Estate, but the tramway company had decided (despite vigorous local opposition) to terminate the line some distance away, at the Trust Inn. Notwithstanding this, the trams came into general service that evening, with a promise of affordable fares in an attempt to encourage long distance travel. Initially, for example, passengers could travel the nine miles from Renfrew to Kilbarchan (via Paisley) for 4d. The terminus itself was eventually re-sited at High Barholm, near Station Road.

The buildings seen here at Low Barholm in 1908 have largely survived. They include the first of several local Co-operative stores (to the right of the photograph, with the bicycle propped against the wall) and, further up on the opposite side of the street, the Trust Inn, whose eastern gable faces the camera. The latter, situated at the bottom end of the village, was designed by Paisley-based architect James Barr for the Renfrewshire Public House Trust Limited, and was officially opened by the latter's chairman, Sir Thomas Glen-Coats, in June 1904. In keeping with the Trust's temperance principles, alcoholic drinks were not on open display within the public bar, and both a family room and a tearoom (the latter serving tea, coffee and cocoa) were provided. Also popular in the village was the well-known Cyclists' Rest, which was located a little further along the street at 4 Low Barholm. This was an Italian café, run for 53 years by Luigi and Giovanella Brunetti, which was famous for its bowls of hot peas soaked in vinegar.

In this view of High Barholm, a No. 43 open-topped Paisley & District tram is sitting at what would eventually become the terminus. To the extreme right of the picture is the Co-operative Buildings, which comprised butchery, drapery and dairy departments. The Kilbarchan Co-operative Society was established in 1872 and, in addition to this building, had a further store across from the Trust Inn (known locally as the 'Low Co'), a cobblers, coal department and stables in Steeple Street, and a grain and provisions store in New Street. In the 1933 Lilias Day Souvenir Programme, it was claimed in a full-page advertisement that the range of goods made by the Scottish Co-operative Wholesale Society Limited (SCWS Limited) 'is so extensive that it is scarcely necessary for you to buy a single article of private manufacture'. In the early 1960s the Kilbarchan Co-operative Society amalgamated with neighbouring Paisley Co-operative Society, but, ultimately, the Co-operative at High Barholm (which was then the village's only remaining Co-operative store) closed. However, around 2004, a new Co-operative store was opened within the building.

This view shows some of the older properties at High Barholm. They include, to the left, the single-storey cottage known as Belltrees, and the then two-storey, but now one-storey, property known as Roselea. Just behind this is a taller three-storey tenement building, which was designed by Paisley-based architect Peter Caldwell and was completed in 1909. Also seen here, sitting at the terminus, is a Glasgow Corporation bus. Following the withdrawal of the Kilbarchan–Elderslie tram service in 1932, and the subsequent introduction of a replacement bus service, the Corporation issued special interchangeable tickets, which were valid on both bus and tram, thus enabling travellers, for example, to purchase one ticket to cover the entire journey from Kilbarchan to Glasgow. A further, and somewhat unusual, facility was the introduction in 1934 of an evening 'postal bus'. This was equipped with a post box, attached to the outside rear of the bus, enabling villagers (whether travelling on the bus or not) to post mail beyond the normal six o'clock deadline. In the mid 1950s, when the Corporation bus service was withdrawn, the route was taken over by Western SMT, and the terminus extended to Wheatlands.

The Liberal Club (with two lamp posts in front of it) and the Baptist Church face each other in this early view of High Barholm. The Liberal Club was designed in the classical style by Glasgow-based architect William Howie, and was formally opened on 23 May 1902 by Sir Thomas Glen-Coats. The ground floor contained a reading room, ladies' room, games room and committee room. The upper floor was taken up by a billiards room, which was warmed by two fires and had a raised platform with seating round the walls for spectators. To the rear of the building, an old weaving shed was converted into a commodious bathroom, with three private baths equipped with hot and cold taps. After the dissolution of the Liberal Club, the building was briefly used as an Adult Centre, but re-opened on December 1953 as a public library. This closed on 18 April 1998, and was replaced with a mobile library service. Later, the property was renovated by the Kilbarchan Improvements Project and is currently a community facility known as The Old Library Centre. Beyond the single-storey cottage, at High Barholm, can be seen the stone pillars that marked the entrance to Spring Grove House.

Spring Grove House (formerly known as Quarry House) dates from the early 1800s and was built just to the west of a small freestone quarry which supplied much of the stone used in the construction of the houses in the village. Amongst its early owners was one John Smith, a partner in the Calton Spinning Company in Glasgow. Originally from Irvine, Mr Smith moved to Spring Grove House and died there in October 1868. He was survived by his twin daughters, Agnes and Margaret, who were also known as the 'sisters of Sinai' due to their discovery, during their travels in the Sinai Peninsula, of early New Testament manuscripts. In September 1921, the then owner (David Morrison) held a public auction at the house. Up for sale were, amongst other things, various breeds of cattle, approximately 1,200–1,500 head of poultry (together with associated brooder house and chicken coops), and a 'varnished governess car'. During the Second World War the house lay empty until temporarily commandeered by the Home Guard. By 1950, however, it was uninhabitable and shortly afterwards was demolished to make way for new housing.

On Saturday 7 May 1904, a large crowd gathered at the foot of Ewing Street to witness the formal opening of the new Kilbarchan Baptist Church by the Rev. Dr Jackson Forbes, vice president of the Baptist Union of Scotland. This Gothic-style church, popularly known as Hunter's Kirk because of its strong personal association with Richard Hunter of Glentyan, was designed by the Glasgow-based architect David Barclay. The church could accommodate 400 people and, in addition, had a hall and a church officer's house. However, after several years of declining membership, it was reluctantly agreed that the church be dissolved from 6 February 1916, with ownership of the building reverting to Richard Hunter. The church was later re-opened as St Barchan's Congregational Church, but in the 1950s this was also closed and the building demolished. In early 1959, a Guide Hall was erected on the site of the church.

In the background of this photograph, taken around 1909, can be seen, on the left, the Baptist Church with its turret (the Steeple is visible in the distance, above the church) and, in the centre, the rear of the Co-operative Buildings in High Barholm. In the foreground is part of the original bowling green of the Kilbarchan Bowling Club, which was located just to the east of Station Road. The Bowling Club was established in 1860 and played here until 1913, when a new green was opened alongside Ladysmith Avenue. The official opening of the new green took place on Saturday, 3 May 1913, and was performed by Sir Thomas Glen-Coats. Despite being an improvement on the old green, some members felt that it was not conveniently situated. As a consequence, they relinquished their club membership and negotiated the lease of the old green, so that, for a few seasons at least, there were two bowling clubs in the village. In May 1960, Kilbarchan Bowling Club celebrated its centenary, opening the green for the season in the presence of representatives from the Scottish Bowling Association, the Renfrewshire Bowling Association, and other invited guests.

Members of Kilbarchan Bowling Club, with guests, *c.* 1900.

Right: On Sunday, 2 October 1921, this slender grey granite war memorial was unveiled by Lord Blythswood and dedicated by local ministers, the Reverends Malcolm Pollock and Robert Mackenzie. Occupying a prominent site at the junction of High Barholm and Station Road, it comprised an octagonal pillar, mounted on an octagonal base, and surmounted by a heraldic Scottish unicorn. Designed by Messrs Wright & Wylie, Glasgow, it was sculpted by Liverpool-born Alexander Proudfoot and erected on site by a local mason, Thomas Gray. Among those present to witness the ceremony were detachments of the 6th Battalion Argyll & Sutherland Highlanders, representatives of the local uniformed organisations, and veterans of the First World War. While pipers played 'The Flowers of the Forest', relatives of those who had lost their lives in the war placed wreaths and flowers around the monument. In 2006, the war memorial was renovated by Renfrewshire Council.

Above: This 1930s view, taken at the foot of Ewing Street (or Steeple Brae, as it was once known), shows another of the decorative arches erected for the Lilias Day celebrations. Like the arch itself, the buildings it is affixed to have now gone – as have most of the older buildings on the right-hand side of the street, between Well Road (the first opening on the right) and the former Clydesdale & North of Scotland Bank at the top of the brae. The latter occupied the building on the corner of Ewing Street and Steeple Square from about 1900 until around 1999, when the bank was closed and the property converted into flats. Among the other businesses on this side of the street in the 1930s were the Co-operative Society's headquarters, cobblers, stables and the hayloft of their Coal Department, as well as Sinclair's tearoom. In the main, the properties on the opposite side of the street have survived, including William Ritchie's (later Adam Marshall's) slater, plasterer and sweep business at 16 Ewing Street.

Left: Undoubtedly, one of Ewing Street's most colourful characters was the weaver Robert Craig. Apparently Robert was, for a period, the village bellman (town crier), although in his case it was the banging of his drum, and not the ringing of a bell, that attracted the attention of the villagers. Seemingly Robert, who died around the turn of the twentieth century, was, like many of the local weaving fraternity, something of a poet in his spare time and he is credited with composing 'Habbie's Dream', a poem about the legendary Kilbarchan piper Habbie Simpson. Another local weaver, Robert Allan, who lived in the 'toonfit' but died in America, had a collection of his own poems published. In 1932, to commemorate his achievements, the Kilbarchan General Society commissioned a fountain bearing an engraving of Robert Allan's head adorned with bay leaves and a few lines of his verse. The fountain is set into a stone wall at the foot of Church Street.

Above: This 1930s view, looking down towards High Barholm, shows the older properties on either side of Ewing Street. These mostly date from the eighteenth and nineteenth centuries and, as can be seen here, were constructed with a stone step at their front doors over the drainage ditch that runs alongside each property. On the extreme left of the photograph is Pirn Cottage. This is presently a private house, but has in the past variously been a tearoom, and a confectioners and tobacconist. At the time of this photograph, it was the Bungalow Tearoom, run by Mrs Kay. Later owners of the tearoom included Mrs Clements and Margaret Semple. In the early 1960s, a second tearoom was opened almost directly opposite by Mrs Janet McSheffrey, in premises which had long been occupied by local provisions merchant, Archibald Buchanan. Earlier (in 1907) there had also been a tearoom in the two-storey building third from right in this photograph. At that time this building was owned by patternmaker, John Millar, but later, in 1921, the tearoom here was run by the Misses Elizabeth and Helen Millar.

Below: In this 1920s photograph, blacksmith George Fulton and apprentice Johnny Lightbody can be seen at the entrance to George's smithy in Steeple Street. George had previously worked in James Martin's smithy in Church Street, but later set up in business on his own. As well as general blacksmithing work, he also repaired and overhauled bicycles and lawnmowers. Kilbarchan's last blacksmith, George retired in the early 1960s when the property containing the smithy was compulsorily purchased, prior to its demolition.

Above: This early 1920s photograph shows Elizabeth Fulton, her husband George (the blacksmith) and their daughter, Betty, at the entrance to Elizabeth's small ironmongery shop, which was situated next door to George's smithy in Steeple Street. In addition to general ironmongery, the shop sold a range of tableware and crystal. The shop closed for business in 1938 and the premises were subsequently converted into a private house. As with the smithy, in the early 1960s, this property was acquired by compulsory purchase, prior to its demolition. The area occupied by both the smithy and the shop is presently vacant ground.

In this view looking up Steeple Street towards the Cross, the entrance to Currie's Pend at number 19 can be seen on the right. This was where a haulage contractor business was established in the mid 1800s by the Currie family – principally to transport finished cloth to the Paisley markets. Within the pend was a store (known locally as the Bundle House) where the hand-woven cloth produced by local weavers was stored prior to transportation. However, as the business expanded, horse-drawn carriages, ranging from simple 'dog carts' to more elegant landaus and Hansom cabs, were made available for public hire. In addition, there were larger horse-drawn brakes for group outings (such as Sunday school trips) and hearses for funerals. The latter ranged from hearses pulled by a single horse (where the coffin was placed under the seats occupied by the mourners) to beautifully decorated glass-sided hearses pulled by a matching team of horses. With the advent of the motor car, the horse-drawn carriages were taken out of service and the family's business further expanded to include the sale of petrol, oil and tyres.

With the possible exception of the restored Weaver's Cottage, the Steeple Building (formerly the Town Buildings) is the most recognisable of the many fine properties which have survived in the village. Built in 1755 on Steeple Knowe by local mason, David Kerr, the Steeple (and a later extension) was funded by James Milliken of Milliken House. Originally a 'meal mercat' (or grain market) and school, the Steeple Building also had a Ladies Room. The latter was initially only for use by female members of the Milliken family to rest between church services, but was eventually opened to all women. The room was later used for library purposes and, finally, for meetings of several of the local Friendly Societies. In 1878, the Steeple Building was sold by the local Kirk Session to John Holmes (a Johnstone-based lawyer) for £100. He, in turn, sold it the following year to the local Parochial Board. In 1894, the property was transferred to Kilbarchan Parish Council and, later, in 1929, to Renfrew County Council. At the time of this photograph (c. 1913), the property was being used to house, among other things, the parish council inspector and collector's office.

Left: Undoubtedly, Kilbarchan's most famous character is Robert Simpson, a local butcher whose nickname 'Habbie' is now applied to anyone born in Kilbarchan. Habbie was the village piper during the 1500s. He had a reputation of being a heavy drinker, and something of a wit. Along with his wife Janet (or Jennie) he is buried in the Old Parish Church graveyard, the grave being marked with their initials and a symbol of a butcher's cleaver. Habbie's life was celebrated in a poem by Robert Sempill of Belltrees. The form of stanza used in this poem later became known as a 'standard Habbie metre', and is said to have influenced Robert Burns. During the annual Lilias Day celebrations, Habbie (represented by someone dressed as him) is ceremoniously brought out of the Steeple in order to pipe the historical procession through the village. Finally, at the end of the day's celebrations, he pipes his last tune and returns to the Steeple once more. At one time in the 1930s, the village's vintage fire tender would be brought out of its storage within the Steeple Buildings and a hose directed on the statue of Habbie, so that his face could be washed in preparation for his Lilias Day appearance.

Right: The true identity of 'Kilbarchan Jock' is somewhat uncertain. He may have been Jock Ritchie, a local weaver who, when he wasn't working at his loom, was involved with the Lanarkshire & Renfrewshire Hunt. His specific role with the Hunt was that of 'runner', working with the terriers used in hunting the fox. Ritchie died in Johnstone in 1918. On the other hand, 'Kilbarchan Jock' could have been William Brodie, who was also known as Heather Jock. Brodie was born in Paisley in 1802 but settled in Bridge of Weir. Brodie had, like Ritchie, been a weaver, but for most of his life Brodie was a wandering beggar, singing and entertaining for his keep. Shortly before his death in 1885, old age prevented him from performing, so he turned to peddling sundry items of haberdashery.

KILBARCHAN JOCK.
A NOTED SCOTCH CHARACTER.

To the extreme left of this pre-1930s view of Steeple Square is Kilbarchan East Church, with the Session House in front of it. In 1786, local discontent with the system of patronage, whereby the minister was chosen not by the congregation but by the local laird, led to a movement to form a breakaway church. A series of public meetings were held in both the old Star Inn, at the foot of Shuttle Street, and the Steeple Building. A preliminary sermon, to assess the amount of interest in the proposed new church, was held on the Steeple Knowe, and proved to be very successful. Further sermons were then held in temporary accommodation until this church, originally named the Kilbarchan Relief Church, was built. The first service was held here on 23 March 1788. Over the years, the church has been altered and expanded, and a session house and hall added. In 1847, when the Relief and Secession churches in Scotland united, the church became a United Presbyterian Church, and later, in 1900, a United Free Church. In 1929, there was a further change as the church took on its present name. The cottages in the centre of the photograph were gifted to Kilbarchan East Church in 1868 and the church hall was built on the site. The house to the extreme right of the photograph is still standing.

Left: Between 1910 and 1920, a baker and confectioner shop owned by a Miss Neilson, and known locally the 'the scone shop', occupied the ground floor of premises at the corner of New Street and Steeple Street. This photograph shows (from left to right) Miss Neilson, her mother, Mary, and shop assistant, Elizabeth Neil, standing in the shop doorway – with a good selection of bakery in the shop window!

The Cross, Kilbarchan.

Above: Until its demolition in the early 1960s, this property occupied a central position on the northeastern corner of Kilbarchan Cross, flanked on either side by New Street (to the left) and Steeple Street (to the right). From the turn of the twentieth century, for a period of at least thirty years, the lower right portion of this property (No. 3, The Cross) housed John Meikle's long-established plumbing and gas fitting business. Another local plumber, Robert Scobie, had premises close by in High Barholm. From the 1940s, until demolition, Meikle's old shop was occupied by confectioner, Annie Paynter, with the shop on the lower left being William Clark's fruit and vegetable shop. The upper portion of the property was housing, which was accessed through a close, the entrance to which is partially hidden by some of the six cloth-capped gentlemen posing in front of the building. The demolition of this property, together with those on either side, was undertaken as part of a road-widening scheme.

Below: This view, taken around 1907, shows older properties on both sides of Steeple Street from the Cross to the Steeple Building. Although many of these were later demolished, some have survived. These include the Masonic Arms (where the lady with the long apron is standing), and the adjacent Black Bull Inn. After the closure of the latter, the premises were occupied for many years by baker and purveyor Geordie Hamilton, one of whose slogans was 'when in Kilbarchan come and have tea here'. The Masonic Arms was, at the time when this photograph was taken, run by John McCuaig, on behalf of its owners, the Masonic Lodge St. Barchan 156. Now a private house, it has also been a printer's shop (run by James Gibb) and an antiques shop.

Left: Mrs Agnes Grant (also known as Polly) in the doorway of the Black Bull Inn. Around 1900, this Inn (known variously as the Bull Hotel, Bull Inn and, latterly, Black Bull Inn) was in the ownership of Agnes.

This photograph shows Dr William Alexander Orr in a horse-drawn buggy outside his Johnstone home. Although Dr Orr's main surgery was located on Johnstone High Street, by 1905 he had opened a second surgery in Steeple Street (by renting a room for this purpose in the Black Bull Inn). It is said that his most commonly prescribed medicine was a concoction known as 'Dr Orr's correction'. Highly regarded locally, Dr Orr died in 1929, aged 74. After his death, local medical services were provided by Dr Dugald Campbell, whose surgery was in the Medical Hall in Ewing Street.

In this view from 1907 we can see, in addition to the Black Bull Inn and the Masonic Arms, two further properties on Steeple Street. The first, to the extreme left of the photograph, is the single-storey building then occupied by grocer and flesher, Robert Ramsay. In addition to this shop at 14 Steeple Street, Robert also had a slaughter house in the adjacent lane, and another shop at 33 High Barholm (which he rented out to milliner Miss Maggie Houston). Robert also owned Over Johnstone Farm, which he farmed when he retired, although he resided at Rosehill on Well Road. Around 1907, and until the Second World War, the Steeple Street shop was occupied by butcher Robert Wylie, and throughout the 1950s and 1960s by another butcher, Robert Ritchie. After the latter's death, the shop was run by his widow, Netta Ritchie, until her retirement in 1962. For many years thereafter, it was a grocers and newsagents, run by Mrs Agnes Irvine. In more recent times (1996), the shop was converted into a dentist's surgery, which it still is today. The second building, to the extreme right of the picture, is now demolished, but then housed Jane M'Oscar's fruit shop and Daniel Maitland's grocery store (seen here advertising 'F. & J. Smith's famed tobaccos and cigarettes').

In this view, looking down Church Street from the Cross, some of the older premises on the left-hand side of the street can be seen. Some of these are still standing, but the building abutting Luchetti's Cross Café has since been demolished. This building was once the property of the Kilbarchan Freemasons Society. Around 1940 it was tenanted by fruiterer, Alex Orr, and later by Miss Currie's sweetie shop. Other traders in Church Street at that time included baker, John Hill, who operated from Nos. 15–17 between 1900 and 1920, and cabinet maker and joiner (and later also undertaker), Andrew Neilson. The building on extreme right of picture is now the Weaver's Cottage. At the time this photograph was taken it actually was a typical weaver's cottage, although after the death of its owner, William Christie, no weaving took place in the cottage. It was latterly occupied by Miss Agnes Christie (from 1930 until 1950), but was scheduled for demolition before she died. However, in 1957, after a long campaign to preserve the cottage, it was handed over to the National Trust for Scotland, in whose care it remains today.

As part of Church Street used to be known colloquially as the 'toonfit' (town foot), the arch seen here, built across the street for the 1934 Lilias Day celebrations, was consequently known as the 'toonfit' arch. However, the route of the historical pageant parade that forms such an important part of the Lilias Day celebrations did not in fact include Church Street in 1934, but there was great competition within the village to see whose arch was the best decorated. In 1934, the responsibility for the construction and decoration of the 'toonfit' arch rested in the hands of a small sub-committee of residents comprising Messrs John Gardner, Colin Houston, George Park and Andrew Neilson.

In this photograph, we see the same arch but from a different perspective, this time looking up towards the Cross. Erected halfway down Church Street, the right-hand column is pinned onto the wall of 19 Church Street, whilst the left-hand side column of the arch is pinned against the stone wall of the Old Parish Church graveyard. Partly visible behind this latter column is one of the round-topped stone pillars that stand at the entrance to the Old Parish Church. Since this photograph was taken, all of the buildings seen further up on the left-hand side of Church Street have been demolished, with the exception of the Weaver's Cottage, whose white-washed gable end can clearly be seen facing camera in this photograph. In the main, these houses had been occupied by weavers, but were largely uninhabitable by 1940. The site of these houses is now the car park for Kilbarchan West Church.

In this view of Church Street, looking north towards the Cross, we can see the entrance to Merchant's Close to the left, and what were possibly the premises of spirit dealer Mrs James Allan directly opposite. Both the Old and New Parish Churches are in the centre of the photograph. The latter, to the left, was designed in the Victorian style by William Howie (who also designed the Liberal Club building at High Barholm). It was opened in January 1901. The erection of the church is said to be largely due to the efforts of its long-serving minister, the

Rev. Robert Mackenzie, who was minister here from 1895 until 1934. In addition to his church work, Reverend Mackenzie served on both the School Board and the local Parish Council, and was the author of a comprehensive parish history published in 1902. Within the church there are five stained glass windows donated in memory of the Cunninghame, Anderson and Glen families, as well as a sixth designed by local artist James Wright.

An early view of the north gable wall of the crow-stepped Category 'B' listed Old Parish Church. This rubble-built church, which dates from 1724, was reputedly erected on the site of an earlier church. In an enclosure to the west of the Old Parish Church are the remains of an earlier chapel dedicated to St Catherine. This chapel was built by Thomas Crawford of Auchenames, following his visit to St Catherine's monastery on Mount Sinai in Palestine. Around 1858, the Old Parish Church was extended and enlarged with the addition of the balustraded square entrance tower by the Kilbarchan-born architect Alexander Kirkland. When the New Parish Church was opened alongside, the Old Parish Church was converted for use as a church hall, and continues to be used for this purpose.

In this 1920s photograph, James Martin's Wallace Grove smithy can be seen at the entrance to Merchant's Close. James, who was in business in the early 1900s, was a general blacksmith and horse shoer. A native of Lanark, he came to Kilbarchan in the 1890s to take over a blacksmith business at the foot of Church Street. He later moved to Merchant's Close and added a motor garage. Also in this picture is Bob Holmes (whose horse-drawn milk cart can be seen to the left of the smithy) and Geordie Fulton, blacksmith, who, on the demise of the Wallace Grove smithy, opened his own smithy and general ironmongers in Steeple Street, opposite the Steeple Building. The Wallace Grove smithy building was eventually demolished around the late 1970s/early 1980s. The other business shown here is the Kilbarchan Motor Company. In later years, this was run by Henry Bethune, who came to Kilbarchan in 1925 after service in the Merchant Navy during the First World War. Henry claimed that he could supply any make of car or motor bike, and also sharpened lawnmowers and charged batteries. He was well known in the village and died in 1959.

A 1920s view of the interior of James Martin's smithy.

In this view of Church Street, taken around 1909, we can again see some of the older surviving properties on the eastern side of Church Street and, opposite, the stone pillars at the entrance to the New Parish Church. These pillars were added in 1792, after the church had been officially opened. Alongside the entrance pillars, and immediately behind the stone wall, are three large flat gravestones, marking the last resting place of Captain James Stirling of Glentyan, his wife, Mary McDowall of Garthland (who died in 1839), and his later wife, Elizabeth Dundas (who died in 1872). The obelisk on the right was erected to commemorate the 49 years of service of the Rev. Robert Graham, who died in 1895.

Glentyan estate included this Georgian-style house, built in the 1780s. Around 1817, the estate was acquired by Captain James Stirling, a distinguished British naval officer. After Stirling's death in 1872, the estate was sold by his Trustees to Thomas Mann, a Glasgow wholesale stationer, who resided at Glentyan until about 1898. Thereafter, the estate was acquired by Richard Hunter, the Chairman and Managing Director of a Glasgow-based wholesale warehousing business. As well as playing a prominent role in local affairs, Richard Hunter was a well-known philanthropist, notably being involved with William Quarrier in establishing the Orphan Homes of Scotland at nearby Bridge of Weir. Richard was also associated with the Glasgow Seamen's Friends Society, and helped to build and equip the Seamen's Bethel in Govan and the Seamen's Institute at the Broomielaw. After Richard's death at Glentyan on 4 April 1939, the estate passed to his son, Charles. Today, the estate is owned by the Stakis family.

The Roarin' Brig, which straddled the Burntshields Road until its demolition in the 1970s, was said to have been built so that the then laird of Glentyan could stroll through his estate without ever having to walk on a public road! At this time, it formed part of the driveway to Glentyan House. The driveway commenced near where Churchill Drive now stands and ended at the main entrance to the house. Although in later years villagers enjoyed a certain freedom to roam the estate, this had not always been the case. In the 1880s, for example, when Glentyan Estate was owned by Thomas Mann, Mann was involved in litigation with two villagers who had claimed that a right-of-way ran through the estate. This celebrated case, 'The Kilbarchan Right-of-Way', reached as far as the House of Lords. Although Mann won his case, he was subsequently required to provide an alternative way through the estate. In the second half of the twentieth century, whilst the Hunter family were in residence, the grounds of Glentyan House were opened to the public on several occasions for fund raising under the Garden Scheme for Scotland.

Left: The so-called Beggars Well, seen here in 1906, was located on the outskirts of Kilbarchan, on the Burntshields Road, and was no more than a stone drinking trough. Although it is likely that it was primarily intended to water horses that were negotiating the steep incline up to the Well, it may also have been used by itinerant beggars (hence the name). During Poor Law times Kilbarchan, like many other small communities in Scotland, did try to provide for local residents who had fallen on hard times, although the parish was reluctant to take responsibility for beggars from outwith the village. In 1830, using monies left nine years previously by George McFarlane of Clippings to provide a facility for needy people, the Old Parish Church Kirk Session opened a poorhouse in the 'toonfit', under the superintendence of Arthur Lang.

Above: The estate of Burntshields (or Burntchells as it was at one time known) is an ancient one, once being held by a family of that name. The house itself, however, is much more recent, probably being built around 1825. For almost all of the last century it has been in the hands of the Marshall family, beginning with Robert Marshall. Robert, who died at Burntshields Farm in his 85th year in November 1935, was said to be a 'notable personality'. A partner in Messrs John Marshall, his firm pioneered tube manufacturing in the east end of Glasgow. Outwith his work, Robert was a noted breeder of hackney horses, some of the best known of which were reared at Burntshields. In addition, he regularly contributed to charities and causes – one being the funding of a new auxiliary hospital for Glasgow's Royal Infirmary. After his death, the estate was inherited by his son, Major Ian Marshall.

THE WEAVERS COTTAGE, KILBARCHAN.

The Weaver's Cottage at the Cross is undoubtedly one of the most well-known properties in Kilbarchan. It was built in 1723 as a workshop and house for John, Andrew and Jenat Brydein (eventually Bryden). It remained in the Bryden family until 1798, when it was sold by Janet and Margaret Bryden to William Brodie. In 1801 it was sold to William Christie and, latterly, was owned by the Christie sisters, but from around 1947 it was under threat of demolition. However, at that time (and a few years before the death of Agnes – who was the last of the Christie sisters) Willie Meikle (a prominent local weaver), with the support of several other like-minded persons, persuaded the National Trust for Scotland to take responsibility for the upkeep of the cottage. It was subsequently gifted to the National Trust by Miss Christie's nephew and niece, Mr and Miss Simpson, and, with the support of local residents, was made into a working museum. It was officially opened in September 1957 by Lord Wemyss, the then Chairman of the National Trust for Scotland.

This view of Shuttle Street, looking towards the Cross, shows the quaintness of the village at the turn of the twentieth century, with its assortment of houses and thatched roof cottages. Like all of the main thoroughfares in the village, Shuttle Street was narrow and unpaved and access to the mainly one and two-storey homes was by means of a raised step under which waste water drained away. Until 1846, when a gasworks was established in the village, there was no street lighting whatsoever. Appropriately, given that the street reputedly took its name from its likeness to the shape of a weaver's shuttle, the occupants of many of the houses in the street were actually weavers. When this photograph was taken, all of the older properties on the right-hand side of the street (with the exception of the workshop of cabinet maker and joiner Andrew Purdon, in Yardshead) were weavers' cottages with one or more working looms.

Shuttle Street arch, Kilbarchan.

In this early 1930s photograph of Shuttle Street, looking towards the Cross, one of five floral arches erected for the 1933 Lilias Day celebrations can be seen straddling the street at Yardshead. This would be one of the last times such an arch was erected here for, in later years, a Clearance Order promoted by the County Council resulted in plans to substantially widen Shuttle Street. In time, all of the properties seen here on the left-hand side of the street were demolished. This same order also affected many of the properties in New Street, including the building seen here with the lantern at the corner of Shuttle Street and New Street. At the time of this photograph, this property was occupied by grocer and provisions merchant, Frances McKenna. Among the buildings in the photograph which survived demolition were the Weaver's Cottage (the north-facing gable wall of which can be seen at the foot of the Shuttle Street) and, diagonally across from the Weaver's Cottage, the buildings long-occupied by both the Black Bull Inn and the Masonic Arms public house.

Fore House, the Georgian-style mansion situated at the top of Shuttle Street, was built in 1773 for John Barbour of Law and, externally at least, remains largely unchanged today. John was the eldest son of Kilbarchan-born Baillie John Barbour (who introduced linen manufacture to the village). He, and his brothers William and Humphrey, inherited the family business in 1770 on their father's death. John was particularly involved in the Irish side of the business, which supervised the import of the good quality flax from Ulster that was used to produce the finished linen cloth. He later settled in Ireland, where he lived out his life. It time, Fore House became part of Richard Hunter's Glentyan Estate and was occupied by Charles Hunter for a period, until the latter took up residence in Glentyan House, on his father's death in 1939. Like other local lairds, the Hunters immersed themselves in the life of the village. In 1935, for example, whilst Charles was presiding over a series of meetings and events to reconstitute and develop the Kilbarchan Unionist Association, his wife was convening a committee set up in conjunction with the Red Cross, to arrange for the collection of clothing to help unemployed people.

For over 400 years, one of the landed families associated with Kilbarchan were the Cunninghames of Craigends. Their estate was situated on the banks of the River Gryfe, near Houston. Their first house (known locally as the 'Old House') was built *c.* 1479 for the first laird, William Cunninghame, who had inherited the estate around this time. Of the numerous succeeding lairds, perhaps the one most closely identified with Kilbarchan was the eighth laird, who was in possession of the estate in 1704 when the village was elevated to a Burgh of Barony. One of the privileges of this elevation was the right to hold annual fair days. One such became known as Lily's Day (and eventually Lilias Day), reputedly after the laird's daughter, Lilias. Around 1856, shortly after the fifteenth laird, Colonel Cunninghame, sold the estate to his uncle, Alexander Cunninghame (Chairman of coal and iron merchants, Merry and Cunninghame), the 'Old House' was demolished. It was replaced with a new house, built nearby, and designed by the Edinburgh-born architect David Bryce, who also designed the iconic Bank of Scotland building on The Mound in Edinburgh.

The new house at Craigends, built in the Scottish Baronial style, had 58 rooms. Now described as his 'lost masterpiece', it was believed to be one of architect David Bryce's best designed country residences. Indeed, interior shots of the house once featured in *Scottish Field*. In 1894, the estate was inherited by the seventeenth and last laird of Craigends, John Cunninghame, who resided there for over 50 years until his death in 1917. Afterwards, the estate passed to his widow, Alison, who lived in the house until her death in 1958. The estate then passed to her nephew, William Cunninghame – however, he was unable to maintain the property and had the contents of the house auctioned off in October 1961. For a number of years thereafter the house lay empty, although the grounds were maintained, giving pleasure to local residents. Gradually, however, the house fell into disrepair, and the final portion was demolished in May 1980. The land was then sold and used for housing.

By 1900, when this photograph was taken, New Street had largely been laid out. At that time, some of the traders operating on the left-hand side of the street were (on the extreme left of the photograph) Miss Stevenson (licensed grocer and spirit dealer), William Barbour (postmaster and draper), Robert Finnie (baker), James and Charles Fraser (tailor and clothier), and, at 25 New Street, John Fraser's Glenleven Inn. On the opposite side of the street was Peter Lyle (bookseller and stationer), one of the several stores of the Kilbarchan Co-operative Society, Hugh Aitken (fruiterer) and Agnes Holmes (newsagent). Shortly after this photograph was taken, William Cook took over Miss Stevenson's shop and continued to operate here until the 1920s. However, by the 1950s, all of these traders had gone, with the exception of the Co-operative store and the post office (then run by John McIntyre). Other businesses at this later time included Tom Barton (barber), John Connell (plumber) and Agnes Irvine (dairy).

From about 1880 until the 1930s, the building to the extreme left of this photograph, and situated on the prime site at the corner of New Street and Shuttle Street, housed a grocers and wine merchants business. The first such proprietor was J. Hall, who was active here in the 1880s. He was followed at the turn of the twentieth century by Patrick Barr (who also had another grocers and wine merchants business at High Barholm). Around 1910, the building was occupied by grocer Duncan Crawford. Remarkably, his was one of four grocers operating at this time in the vicinity of the Cross – a far cry from the situation in later years. By 1930, another grocer, Frances McKenna, was the tenant of the building. Later, during the Second World War, the shop lay empty, but from the 1950s and until demolition the shop was occupied by James Ritchie and then by Allan M. Campbell & Son (both butchers).

New Street Arch, Kilbarchan.

In this 1930s view, looking back towards the Cross, New Street is framed with one of the Lilias Day arches. The New Street arch was always the fifth and final arch passed under during the Lilias Day Parade, as it made its way to the Public Park. As can be seen, the old properties in the street were largely intact at the time this photograph was taken. However, most have now been demolished. The exceptions are the Glenleven Inn (situated on the right-hand side of the street, near the parked car nearest to camera), which has been in existence since at least 1901, and (on the opposite side of the street) the property which housed painters Thomas Gould & Sons, and for a period served as a base for both Glentyan Thistle Football Club and Kilbarchan Harriers.

The Lilias Day procession in New Street, 1931.

Gateside Place, Kilbarchan

All of the two-storey properties seen here in Gateside Place date from the 1860s. They were built for weavers and their families and had weaving rooms on the ground floor and living accommodation above. All the properties are today, externally, largely unchanged. Just visible alongside the south-facing gable end of No. 9 (at the foot of the street and facing the camera) is a narrow lane, with high stone walls on either side, which leads into Kilbarchan Public Park. The stone wall in the foreground to the extreme right of the photograph now leads to Old School Square, a modern development that stands on the site of an old school for females. This school was ultimately used (until 1958) as a dining room for nearby Kilbarchan Primary School. Although Gateside Place was mostly residential, both William Borland (slater) and John Connell (plumbers and gasfitter) at one time had businesses in the cul-de-sac. The latter, whose business was originally in New Street, relocated to Gateside Place in the late 1950s.

Prior to the opening of the school at Meadside in New Street, local children either attended the Parish School within the Steeple Hall or the Female Charity School in New Street. Initially, the then recently appointed Kilbarchan & Houston School Board had intended that the new school be built on the Butt Meadows. However, the estimated cost of £5,000 was deemed to be too high and, accordingly, the Meadside site was chosen instead. The official opening of the school took place on 22 October 1877. Its first headmaster was the redoubtable Thomas McCrorie, who retired in 1927 at the age of 79, having served as headmaster for fifty years. From 1896 onwards, the school was extended on several occasions – notably in 1940 when a new Infants Department was opened. Although the school had taken students up to and including junior secondary level, it eventually became solely a primary school in 1956. Over the years, with an ever-increasing school roll, temporary huts were erected to provide much-needed extra accommodation. Finally, in June 1990, Kilbarchan Primary School was closed and replaced with a new school in Meadside Avenue. Today, modern housing has been built on the site of the old Primary School.

Kilbarchan Public Park was officially opened on 1 September 1888 by Dr Barbour of Gryffe. The mounds within the park were said to have been constructed using waste coal from nearby pits. These are known locally as the 'big hill' and the 'wee hill' – both popular with sledging enthusiasts during the winter months. Some seven years after the park was opened, this splendid grey granite public fountain was installed. Known locally as the Orr Fountain, it was officially unveiled on 19 October 1895 and was the gift of John Orr, who was born in Kilbarchan in 1834. During his early working life, Orr was apprenticed to a baker, however he emigrated to New Zealand in 1857. After about 25 years at sea, serving as ship's cook, Orr opened dining rooms in Wellington, New Zealand, including the well-known Wellington City Buffet Hotel. The fountain, although still *in situ*, is no longer operational. In the background, to the left, is Meadowbank. This was once the home of local draper William Crawford. To the right, beyond the park, are the former weavers' houses at Park View.

The estate of Milliken, formerly Johnstoune, was acquired by Ludovic Houston around 1650. It was sold by one of his sons to Major James Milliken, a wealthy West Indies sugar merchant, in 1733. Almost immediately, Major Milliken demolished the existing house (known as Johnstone Castle) and replaced it with the newer and grander Milliken House, seen here. One particular feature of this new house was the formal gardens which contained a series of waterfalls and artificial ponds, created by diverting the Kilbarchan Burn which ran through the estate. Sadly, this house was later destroyed by fire. As a consequence, in 1830 the then owner, Sir William Napier, built another elegant mansion. In May 1886, the link with the Napier family was broken when, during the tenure of Sir Robert Napier, the estate, together with mansion house, policies and adjoining farms, was put up for public sale. The new owner, Archibald McKenzie, remained in possession until 1921, when it was acquired by the well-known Scottish architect, George Boswell, who demolished Milliken House.